THE STRANGE *and* LONELY

VINCENT VA

Written by Jenny Alexander
Illustrated by Olivia Bown

Collins Educational
An imprint of HarperCollins*Publishers*

Contents

List of Paintings

Introduction

Vincent van Gogh died in 1890 when he was 37 years old. During his short life, he produced over 800 paintings, but only ever managed to sell one.

Like his paintings, van Gogh was misunderstood and rejected by many of the people around him because he wasn't interested in the same things as them. Money, success, clothes and fashion – these were not important to him at all. But he had great passion, faith and honesty which shine through the story of his unusual life, just as they shine through his paintings.

Self-portrait, 1887. Oil on canvas 41 x 35.5cm.

A Most Unusual Boy

Vincent van Gogh was born on 30 March, 1853 in Groot Zundert in the Netherlands, the eldest of six children; three sisters and two brothers. By a strange coincidence, his mother had given birth to a stillborn baby boy exactly a year before, and as her second son shared his dead brother's birthday, she gave him the same names as well – Vincent Willem van Gogh.

It must have been odd for Vincent as he grew up, to see his own name and birthday on his brother's tombstone, beside the church where his father was pastor.

Vincent was a solitary boy, who spent much of his time alone, taking long walks in the countryside. He rarely played with the other children in the village, even his own younger brother and sisters.

At school, he didn't do very well, and he didn't even show much promise in his art classes, although his mother had taught him how to draw at home. So when he was 13, his father decided to send him away to boarding school, to see if he would do any better there.

But Vincent missed his family so much that he was too miserable to work and he didn't find it easy to make friends. His father moved him to a second boarding school. When that didn't seem to make him any happier, it was decided that he should leave school, at the age of 15, to start a career.

A Young Man in London

Vincent van Gogh's uncle, also called Vincent, had a business selling works of art in several European countries. He gave Vincent a job as an art dealer in The Hague. The young man did well. He did so well, in fact, that after five years he was given the chance to work for the company in London as a reward. He was 20 years old.

Vincent liked London and at first he was very happy there. He learned to speak English fluently, and his passion for art and literature grew. For the first time in his life, he fell in love. He was so shy, however, he couldn't tell the girl he loved her. He just brooded about it. Eventually, he couldn't keep it secret any more, but by that time, it was too late – the girl had fallen in love with someone else.

Vincent was bitterly disappointed. He lost interest in everything, and his work began to suffer. He began to tell his customers not to buy the paintings he personally didn't like or thought were too expensive. When his uncle found out, Vincent was dismissed.

For a short time, Vincent became a school teacher. One of his tasks was to collect school fees. But he was so upset by the poverty of some of the families he visited, he couldn't bring himself to ask them for any money. He gave up teaching, and following his growing interest in religion, he decided to become a preacher instead.

Coming Home to the Church

Vincent's father was delighted that his son had decided to follow him into the church. He arranged for Vincent to come home and train properly as a lay preacher. Vincent didn't enjoy the studies, and after three months he was told he had failed the course. Luckily he wasn't interested in getting a well-paid job in the church and a position in the community. What Vincent wanted was to get on with what he saw as the real work, helping poor people and bringing them the word of God.

He managed to get a position as a lay preacher in the Borinage, a desperately poor area of Belgium, where he lived among the miners and their families. He gave away all his warm clothes and most of his food, and made himself the poorest among the poor. This was what he thought God wanted him to do.

It wasn't what the church leaders wanted, though. They thought Vincent looked so thin and ragged that he was a disgrace to himself and to them. So they stopped paying him at all. He had to survive on charity for the next two years. During this time, he made many drawings, and when he returned, exhausted, from the Borinage, he had a new ambition – he would become an artist. He wrote to his brother, Theo, that he hoped he would be able to express his love of God in his painting. "Art is worship," he said, "inasmuch as it places beauty (which is the same thing as Goodness) in the heart of Man."

First Steps in Painting

In 1880, Vincent went to the Academy of Fine Art in Brussels for a year. Theo, who was now working in their uncle Vincent's art business, began to send him money to live on, out of his own salary, and did so for the rest of Vincent's life.

When Vincent went home again, his parents welcomed him. They were pleased. He seemed to have started on a good career at last and Vincent worked hard and energetically at his painting. But very soon, there was more trouble. Vincent fell in love again. This time the girl was his cousin, Kee, who was staying at the house. Unfortunately, she didn't feel the same way about him and she became so tired of his declarations of love that she went back to Amsterdam. He followed her there, but she refused even to see him. He was so disappointed, he held his left hand in a candle flame and burned it, in a desperate attempt to show her parents how serious he was about her. In the end, however, he was forced to give up and return home.

By now, living at home was more difficult. Vincent was still upset about Kee, and he and his father quarrelled much of the time. At Christmas time, after a particularly violent argument, he left home and travelled to The Hague.

The Hague

While he was in The Hague, Vincent met the third great love of his life. She was a poor woman called Sien. She already had one child and was pregnant with another. Vincent moved in with her and they planned to marry. Vincent's family were unhappy about this, as it was wrong in the eyes of the Church, for a man and a woman to live together without being married. Also, the money Theo could afford to send was not enough to support Vincent, Sien and the two children. They often had to go hungry. In the end, Theo had to warn Vincent that his family might commit him to a mental hospital unless he chose between Sien and his art. Vincent left Sien and her children and travelled to Drente, alone, to think about his future and his work.

Drente – A Time for Thought

Vincent was thirty years old. In an extraordinary letter to his brother, he wrote that he only expected to live another six to ten years. He wasn't concerned if he had a short or long life, so long as he could leave something worthwhile behind. He was ready to put thoughts of romantic love and family life behind him, and devote all his energy and passion to his work.

I not only began drawing relatively late, but in addition I may well not have so very many years of life ahead of me .....

As far as the time that remains for my work is concerned, I believe that I can assume that this body of mine will still keep going despite everything, for a certain number of years yet – say, between six and ten. I do not intend to spare myself or pay much heed to moods or problems — it is a matter of some indifference to me whether I have a longer or a shorter life, and in any case, physical molly coddling such as a doctor can accomplish is not to my taste .....

The Making of an Artist

When Vincent decided he didn't want to be on his own anymore, he returned, yet again, to his family home. His father had been given a new living at Neunen by his church, and Vincent stayed there for two years – the longest period he spent anywhere in his adult life.

He worked hard, copying pictures by great artists, and painting scenes from the surrounding area. These early paintings were dark and sombre. He often used only a few colours, mostly dull browns and greens. As well as landscapes, he also painted poor people going about their work. He thought of himself as a simple labourer, practising his craft to perfection.

Vincent wrote, "painting is a faith," and, "let us try to master technique so well that people are deceived and say we have no technique". He didn't want to be famous and wealthy and he didn't even sign his full name on his pictures. He simply signed them, 'Vincent'.

It soon became clear to Vincent's father that his son would never tidy himself up and become famous, and he began to lose patience with him. People in the village were unhappy having someone who could behave so strangely living among them, and people in the Church disapproved of his mixing with tramps and the non-believers.

Vincent, for his part, found his father cold-hearted and too worried about keeping up appearances. He thought that, as a pastor, his father should be more interested in helping the poor and less keen to further his own career. They had many arguments, and Vincent often became very angry and depressed about them.

In the spring of 1885, Vincent's father had a stroke and died. Although they had always had such a stormy relationship, it affected Vincent deeply.

In the difficult weeks after his father's death, he painted what is now considered to be his first real masterpiece, *The Potato Eaters.*

Vincent chose to paint poor people, with nothing to eat but potatoes, because he felt very close to them, and he wanted to show wealthy people how the poor lived. Throughout the summer, he did a series of paintings of peasants working in the fields, and in the autumn he painted still-lifes of bowls and baskets of potatoes. Shortly afterwards, he left The Hague, never to return.

Self-portrait Before
His Easel, 1888.
Oil on canvas 65 x 50.5cm

Woman Digging

Canvas on panel, 42 x 32cm
Neunen, August 1885
Barber Institute, Birmingham

Van Gogh wrote in a letter, "Peasants digging are closer to my heart, and I have found things better outside paradise, where the literal meaning of 'the sweat of his brow' becomes apparent..." The dark colours and heavy brush strokes reflect the labour and toil of the woman's life, and the ground is hard and rocky, and the sky grey, offering little hope.

Head of a Peasant Woman

Oil on canvas
Neunen, April 1885
National Gallery of Scotland

Another early picture where he used the same dark colours, picking out the subject with a dull, whitish tone. Another dominant colour is blue, which is found both in her headdress and her dress. He said, "I am always looking for blue... The people here instinctively wear the most beautiful blue I have ever seen."

Paris – Two Brothers Together

Vincent decided to go to Paris, because it was the most exciting place for a painter to be at that time. There was a group of artists, known as the Impressionists who were experimenting with new ways of using colours and materials, and Vincent wanted to see their pictures for himself.

By now, Theo was working in the Paris branch of his uncle's business, so when Vincent arrived in the city without warning, Theo took him in. At first, they found living together quite difficult. Vincent's health was beginning to fail, and his behaviour was moody and unpredictable. Theo, being a successful businessman, had a respectability Vincent despised.

But things soon settled down, and their relationship, which had always been based on family loyalty, gradually changed to become one of great warmth and friendship. Theo found that there were two sides to Vincent's nature – the generous, sensitive, kind side, and the selfish, tempestuous, unpredictable one.

"It is as if two people dwelt within him," he complained, "one of them marvellously talented, the other selfish and hard-hearted."

Theo introduced Vincent to some of the established artists who had pictures in his uncle's gallery, Vincent, in his turn, introduced Theo to the struggling younger artists he was mixing with. The two brothers lived together so successfully that by the time Vincent left, Theo felt confident that Vincent would one day become famous and respected as an artist.

"When he arrived here 2 years ago," Theo wrote to his sister, "I would never have thought that we could become so close. Now I am on my own again, I feel the emptiness in my home all the more. It is not easy to fill the place of a man like Vincent. His knowledge is vast and he has a very clear view of the world. I am convinced that if he has a few more years he will make a name for himself."

French Street Scene, Watercolour.

Van Gogh and the Impressionists

Vincent met the Impressionist painters while he was in Paris. Many of them, including Monet, Renoir, Degas and Pissarro, sold their pictures in Theo's gallery.

The Impressionists rejected the traditional way of painting by mixing the colours on the palette and painstakingly building a picture that looked exactly like the subject. Instead, they tried to give an impression of what they were painting by using dashes of pure colour, and leaving the details to the imagination. Using this technique, they could complete their pictures very rapidly, which appealed to Vincent

Vincent also liked the Impressionists' idea of painting out of doors whenever possible, so that they could see the landscape as they worked, instead of making sketches and working from them back in the studio.

The Impressionists didn't use black because they didn't think it was a true colour and Vincent, too, gradually moved away from the blacks and dark browns of his earlier work. He also moved away from his need to make moral statements in his painting.

But Vincent didn't just copy the Impressionists' methods; he put them together with other styles of painting he admired and so produced a new style that was all his own. Japanese art was his other main influence. He adopted the bold use of dark outlines and flat expanses of colour used by Japanese artists, reintroducing black, but combining it with bright colours now, to make a really dramatic effect.

Vincent worked day and night. Art was his passion, the only thing that mattered to him. Sometimes he didn't eat, and if he had money, he would often give it away to people even poorer than he was himself. He couldn't discuss art without getting into arguments because he felt so strongly about it; and he wasn't interested in talking about anything else. Pissarro, one of the oldest Impressionists, told him that he would either go mad or leave the rest of the Impressionists far behind.

Restaurant de la Sirène at Asnières

Oil on canvas, 53 x 65cm
Paris, Spring 1887
Ashmolean Museum, Oxford

This picture follows the Impressionist method of painting, using dashes of pure colour, but avoiding using black, to give an impression of the scene the artist is looking at. Vincent painted it in the springtime, and the season is vividly expressed by the fresh pale green and yellow, and the paleness of the sky.

DE LA SIRENE

The Italian: Agostina Segatori

Oil on canvas, 81 x 60cm
Paris, December 1887
Musee d'Orsay, Paris

Vincent used a pattern of lines on the chair back, and around the edges of this picture, for purely decorative effect. The feeling of depth is achieved not by shading, in the traditional way, but by the use of pattern and outlines. These are techniques taken from Japanese art, but used in a different way, with the paint applied so thickly that the brush-marks show. This method is called 'impasto'.

The Post Impressionists

Vincent and his young friends were called the 'side-street artists' because their work did not sell well and the established galleries were not interested in exhibiting them. They were experimenting with the successful Impressionist formula, but trying to develop their work in new ways, and their ideas had not caught on yet.

Among these Post-Impressionists were Cézanne, Seurat, Toulouse Lautrec and Gauguin. Some of them found it too expensive to continue living in Paris when they couldn't sell their work, so they moved away. Gauguin went to Normandy and van Gogh went south because he had decided that the South of France was similar to Japan in appearance. He wrote, "Japanese painting is highly regarded, all the Impressionists are influenced by it; why then should one not go to Japan, or a reasonable copy – the South?"

The South of France

When Vincent arrived in Arles in the spring of 1888, he found the countryside covered in snow. But soon the fruit trees blossomed, and he took this as a sign that he had been right to move – blossom featured strongly in the Japanese paintings he loved so much. He threw himself into painting pictures of the orchards and felt happy that he was too poor to furnish his room properly, as he knew the Japanese created the paintings he so admired in bare rooms.

When he had built up such a collection of new paintings that he needed somewhere to store them, he rented "the yellow house" in Arles. Yellow, in Japan, was the colour of friendship, and Vincent, again, took this as a good omen – he was hoping to set up an artists' colony there. He asked Gauguin to join him and after first refusing, Gauguin finally agreed when Theo offered to pay his fare. Vincent had been on his own for nine months and he looked forward to Gauguin's arrival with growing excitement. He worked furiously. If it was windy, he pinned the corners of his canvas down with stones. If it was dark, he put lighted candles across the top of his easel and around the brim of his hat. He painted landscapes, seascapes and buildings, still-lifes, portraits and flowers. One of his most famous paintings, *Sunflowers*, was painted at this time, to brighten the walls of his studio.

Sunflowers

Oil on canvas, 93 x 73cm
Arles, August 1888
National Gallery, London

Van Gogh planned to do a series of a dozen pictures of sunflowers, to decorate his yellow house at Arles. He started each painting at dawn to make sure they were finished within a day, before the sunflowers wilted. The picture is almost completely made up of yellow and gold, the colour of friendship and light. Vincent said the flowers glowed like stained glass, with the light shining through it.

Vincent

Living with Gauguin

At first, the two painters got on well, living companionably. However, after a few weeks they began to argue and Gauguin wrote to Theo that he would have to return to Paris because of "temperamental incompatibility". Things became steadily worse, and after two months, Vincent realised that Gauguin would soon decide to leave. It was then he painted *Vincent's Chair with His Pipe,* which expresses the solitary existence to which he would soon be returning.

Vincent's Chair

Oil on canvas, 93 x 73.5cm
Arles, 1888
National Gallery, London

The dark outlines of the chair are 'coloured in' with fairly flat areas of yellow. The paint is applied so thickly that the brush strokes are clearly visible, especially on the floor and the green wall behind.

Vincent

Gauguin and Vincent could discuss all sorts of things, except the one subject that mattered most to both of them – art. Their views were so different that they always ended up arguing. Gauguin often criticised Vincent's work, which was particularly hard on Vincent as he still wasn't making any money, and Gauguin's pictures were just beginning to sell.

Things erupted on the night of 23 December, when they had a violent quarrel over the work of Rembrandt, and Vincent threatened Gauguin with violence.

Gauguin decided to leave and spent the next day packing his bags. Vincent was extremely upset and came at Gauguin with a razor, causing him to flee the house in terror.

Vincent's Madness

After Gauguin had left, Vincent, in a fit of madness, cut off the lobe of his left ear. He washed it carefully, put it in an envelope, and gave it as a present to a woman he knew in the village with the words, "Keep this object safe." Then he went home to bed.

The next day, the townspeople alerted the police that there were mysterious goings-on at the yellow house. The police found Vincent suffering from hallucinations and loss of blood, and they took him to hospital.

Theo came to see him as soon as he heard what had happened, and Vincent began to recover. He painted two pictures of himself with a bandaged ear and a portrait of his doctor, by way of thanks. He described his illness to Theo as "an artist's fit" and sent warm greetings to Gauguin.

When he seemed well enough, he returned to the yellow house, but after only ten days was re-admitted to hospital believing that someone was trying to poison him, and hearing voices. After his second return to the yellow house, he found that many of his neighbours had signed a petition asking the mayor to have "the red-headed madman" taken back to hospital again. Still suffering from bouts of weakness and sleepless nights, Vincent decided he was unable to take care of himself and went, voluntarily, to a mental hospital for a while to try to regain his strength.

Self-Portrait with Bandaged Ear

Oil on canvas, 60 x 49cm
Arles, January 1889
Courtauld Institute Galleries, London

Vincent painted this portrait in the brief period of calm between cutting off his ear and going into the mental hospital. The brush strokes, which are nearly all going the same way, from top to bottom, express this calmness and control, as does the tranquil Japanese print in the background.

In the Hospital at St Remy

Vincent admitted himself to the mental hospital at St Remy, a village 16 kilometres from Arles. Sometimes he had fainting fits and terrifying hallucinations, and sometimes he couldn't sleep at night. During further attacks, he even tried to harm himself by eating poisonous paints and drinking kerosene. The only treatment he was given was a cold bath twice a week. But whenever he could, he worked.

At first, he was only allowed out into the hospital grounds, but later on he went into the countryside, watched over by a member of the hospital staff. In just over a year, he produced 200 paintings. They are works of huge energy and power. For Vincent had given up every last hope of fitting in with other people, and was ready to follow his own extraordinary talent wherever it led him. Vincent had suffered all his life because he didn't conform with those around him. Even though he had been rejected by the Church and misunderstood by his family, his friends and other artists, his immense need to paint never left him.

The other constant in his life was the devoted support of his brother. Even though Theo was now married, he still paid all Vincent's hospital fees and provided his paints and materials. And he went on believing in Vincent's work, sure that one day other people would start to appreciate it, too.

Then, in February 1890, one of Vincent's pictures was sold by a gallery in Brussels for 400 francs. Theo was both delighted and relieved. His wife had just given birth to a baby boy, called Vincent Willem after his uncle, and he knew that with more mouths to feed at home, it was bound to get harder for him to go on supporting Vincent.

Self-Portrait

Oil on canvas, 65 x 54cm
St Remy, 1889
Musee d'Orsay, Paris

All the energy and fire of the artist shows in this painting, in the swept-back hair, fiery-red beard and piercing eyes. The swirling brush strokes of the background spread down across his jacket, filling the canvas with movement and restlessness.

Cornfield with Cypresses

Oil on canvas
July 1889
National Gallery, London

During his time in hospital, van Gogh painted many pictures of cypress trees. “The cypresses occupy me continually,” he wrote. Here, the trees stand against a huge sky of swirling greens and blues. The hills and bushes have dark outlines, but they are painted with the same curling brush strokes, as are the cypresses themselves. The whole picture moves like a restless ocean.

Going North Again

As Vincent recovered, he began to think about his Dutch homeland, and draw sketches from memory of the countryside he grew up in. He decided to go north again, but he didn't go back to The Hague. He took Theo's advice and went to Auvers, a town to the north of Paris, where Theo knew a doctor who was prepared to keep an eye on him. His name was Doctor Gachet. He worked in Paris three days a week. He was friends with some of the Impressionists and liked to paint in his spare time. He was also a great admirer of Vincent's work.

Within a month of Vincent's arrival in Auvers, Dr Gachet told Theo he was confident that Vincent had made a full recovery and there was no risk of a relapse. But at the same time as Vincent was recovering, Theo had financial worries and his health was suffering. He had a bad cough and looked thin and tired. When Vincent visited Theo in Paris, he worried about him, but was unable to stay long. Vincent wrote to Theo, saying how sorry he was to be such a burden, and how sad he was to see him in such difficulties. Vincent referred to "the hours I shared with you which were a bit too difficult and trying for us all. It was no slight thing, when we all felt our daily bread was in danger..." Vincent felt that if he were dead, his paintings would begin to sell and Theo's troubles would soon be over.

Despite all this, Vincent carried on painting big pictures of windswept fields and stormy skies. Then one evening a few weeks later, without any warning, he went out into the countryside and shot himself in the chest. He didn't die but managed to walk home and put himself to bed. His landlady, seeing that he was injured, sent for the local doctor and Dr Gachet. They couldn't get the bullet out, so they made him as comfortable as they could, and the next morning, Dr Gachet sent for Theo.

Theo came immediately. All day he sat by his brother's bedside, while Vincent, propped up on his pillows, lay smoking his pipe. It was early the next morning when Vincent died. The last thing he said to Theo was that he wished it was all over. He was only 37 years old.

They laid him in a coffin and put his easel, stool and painting materials beside it. They covered it in flowers – especially sunflowers which Vincent loved so much. But the priest would not let them use the town's hearse to carry his body to the graveyard, because he had committed the sin of suicide. So they had to borrow a hearse from a neighbouring town.

He was buried in the cemetery at Auvers, surrounded by wheatfields and with the wide, blue sky above. Dr Gachet told the friends gathered at the graveside that Vincent had been a honest man and a great artist. He cared about people and he cared about art and he would live on, in his paintings.

Theo

Theo was heartbroken by Vincent's death, and saddened that his dream of the great things they might achieve together was gone. His health continued to fail and he died six months later. He was buried beside Vincent in the cemetery at Auvers.

Some Important Dates

1852	30 March – birth and death of Vincent Willem, first child of Cornelia and Pastor Theodorus van Gogh.
1853	30 March – birth of Vincent Willem van Gogh in Groot Zundert, first surviving child.
1857	Birth of Theodorus van Gogh.
1869	Vincent goes to work in his uncle's art business in The Hague.
1873	Transfers to the London office.
1876	Becomes a school teacher in England, and then a preacher.
1878	Travels to the Borinage, in Belgium, to preach.
1880	Decides to become an artist.
1882	Rows with his father and goes to The Hague. Theo starts sending him money from his own salary.
1883	Goes to Drente, then returns to his parents home, which is now in Neunen.
1885	Death of Vincent's father. Vincent leaves The Hague.
1886	Goes to Paris, where he lives with Theo.
1888	Goes to Arles and spends nine months alone, before being joined by Paul Gauguin. After a violent quarrel with Gauguin, he cuts off part of his ear.
1889	Goes to the mental hospital at St. Remy.
1889	Birth of Theo's son, Vincent Willem.
1890	Vincent moves to Auvers. He shoots himself in the chest and dies two days later.
1891	Theo dies.

Pronouncing the Dutch Words

People		Places	
Van Gogh	*Van Gof*	Groot Zundert	*Crote Zerndert*
Kee	*Kay*	Neunen	*Nernen*
Sien	*Seen*	Drente	*Drenter*
		The Hague	*The Hayg*

Pronouncing the French Words

People		Places	
Gauguin	*Go-gan*	The Borinage	*The Borinarj*
Dr Gachet	*Dr Gashay*	Arles	*Arl*
Auvers	*Ovair*		

Map

The map below shows the places
van Gogh lived.

London, The Hague, Groot Zundert, Neunen, Drente,
The Borinage, Brussels, Paris, Auvers, Arles, St. Remy.

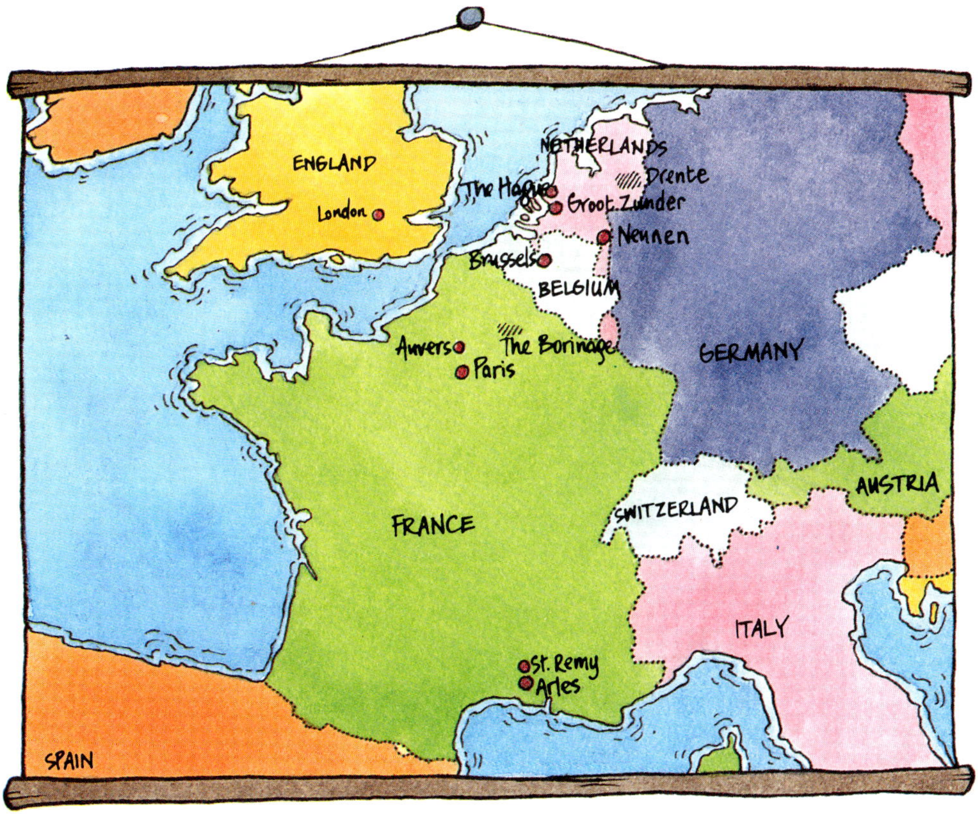

Acknowledgements

Self Portrait, 1887 by Vincent van Gogh, (1853-90)
Musee d'Orsay, Paris/Bridgeman Art Library, London
Credit Giraudon/Bridgeman Art Library

Self Portrait before his Easel, 1888 by Vincent van Gogh, (1853-90)
Rijksmuseum Vincent Man Gogh, Amsterdam/Bridgeman Art Library, London
Topham Picture Source, Edenbridge

Woman Digging by Vincent van Gogh, 1853-90)
Barber Institute, Birmingham/Bridgeman Art Library, London

Head of a peasant woman, 1885 by Vincent van Gogh, (1853-90)
National Gallery of Scotland, Edinburgh/Bridgeman Art Library, London

French Street Scene by Vincent van Gogh, (1853-90)
Private Collection/Bridgeman Art Library, London

Restaurant de la Sirène at Asnières, 1887 by Vincent van Gogh, (1853-90)
Musee d'Orsay, Paris/Bridgeman Art Library, London
Credit Giraudon/Bridgeman Art Library

The Italian: Agostina Segatori by Vincent van Gogh, (1853-90)
Musee d'Orsay, Paris/Bridgeman Art Library, London
Credit Giraudon/Bridgeman Art Library

Sunflowers, 1888 by Vincent van Gogh, (1853-90)
National Gallery, London/Bridgeman Art Library, London
Credit Index/Bridgeman Art Library

Vincent's Chair, 1888 by Vincent van Gogh, (1853-90)
Tate Gallery, London/Bridgeman Art Library, London

Self Portrait with Bandaged Ear, 1889 by Vincent van Gogh, (1853-90)
Courtauld Institute Galleries, Univ. of London/Bridgeman Art Library, London

Self Portrait, 1889 by Vincent van Gogh, (1853-90)
Musee d'Orsay, Paris/Bridgeman Art Library, London
Credit Giraudon/Bridgeman Art Library

Cornfield with Cypresses, July 1889 by Vincent van Gogh, (1853-90)
National Gallery, London/Bridgeman Art Library, London